Break Free!

(Becoming a Forgiving Person)

Ray W. Lincoln

ISBN: 978-0-9961208-0-7
LCCN: 2015934250
Printed in the United States of America
Apex Publications
Littleton, CO

"Live free or die."
Motto of the State of New Hampshire

"Forgive or be chained to the stake of hurt."
Ray W. Lincoln

4

Contents

Preface

"Why can't I forget what has been done to me? I think I'd like to be a forgiving person but I'm stuck. Yes, and with no way that I can see to extricate myself from all my anger and resentment. P.S. It's all justified anger, of course."

"It was a long time ago when I was hurt by the one I thought was my best and trustworthy friend," complained Jason. "He still haunts me, or something does, and I've tried all the advice that well-meaning friends and counselors have thrown my way, but I can't seem to be released from the pain. My whole life is being shaped by a hurt I keep trying to forget."

Sound familiar? Your story is different, no doubt, but is forgiveness still a problem for you too? Does the hurt of some past offense still rise to trouble you?

To ask why this book was conceived and written is like asking "Are we human?" Both should be poignantly obvious. And this book attempts to address the subject of forgiveness from a different point of view: our core temperament. If we are ever going to find the best way to motivate and heal ourselves we will have to pay attention to how we are designed, how we function — our innerkinetics. This book will do that and more.

More secrets to our self-motivation and our ability or willingness to forgive are found in the understanding of our temperament than people think. More therapists are beginning to realize that we are helped best when our own unique inner selves are taken into account.

I don't like long prefaces so let's move on — and moving on is forgiveness at its core.

To your freedom from hurt!
Ray W. Lincoln

Introduction

"It still riles me big time!   Every time I back out of the garage and see what that slimy coward did to the trees I planted on the boundary line, I feel the rage return and my whole day turns sour.   I could kill him!   Well, you know what I mean: cutting them off at fence level and removing all my back yard privacy — and doing it while we were away on vacation and after I had asked him to keep a watch on our house while we were gone.   It makes me madder than...   Well, I'd love to stick a nest of hornets in his pants!"

"I've had what feels like panic attacks at night when I think about him," Clyde continued.   "I can't stop thinking about what he did.   If I go out for a nice meal, my mind returns to the loss of my privacy and the sight of those naked tree stumps, and the steak tastes like cardboard.   When I come home at night after work, there they stand, taunting me, and that rat is secluded somewhere in his house.   It was the house of my friend, I thought, and now I can't look at it without feeling like throwing up.   I walk in the house each night angry and upset and my wife is getting sick of the bad blood that throbs in my veins.   Can't someone help me?"

We can get stuck in our hurts like Clyde — so stuck that all the general advice does no good.   If forgiveness will free us, shouldn't there be a rush on forgiveness?   Hardly. Forgiveness seems as though we are letting the rotten, immoral criminals that hurt us off the hook or glossing over their responsibility to be accountable, as one temperament in particular would see it.   And this temperament's cry for justice is not unwarranted.   What do those who long for human

9

kindness do when people get away with wrong? It feels so right to be resentful and angry.

We can get unstuck. We can do it without sacrificing our strong feelings and values if we understand forgiveness correctly and use the strengths we have been given. Who we are at the core will have a lot to do with how we remain stuck or how we free ourselves from the prisons of hurt, anger, resentment, and the solitary confinement of bitterness. Our *innerkinetics* (inner powers) will be our guide to freedom and healing.

Our journey will be…
- To introduce ourselves to temperament and to the core strengths it gives us — to discover the role our strengths can play in helping us forgive.
- To discover how weaknesses are made and see the part they can play in our inability to release ourselves from our hurts and grievances.
- Then temperament by temperament, we'll find how we can best handle our grievances and let them go. We could call this finding solutions that are driven and motivated by the intelligent use of our strengths, and we would be right.
- Finally, a word about the principle lessons we have hopefully learned.

Before you read on, complete the Adult Temperament Key and follow the instructions to identify your temperament. You can find it in Appendix One.

To conserve your time and energy, much of the text has been presented in bullet form. Each bullet point is meant to make you think and flesh out its meaning so that you "make it your own" and buy into the process of learning how to forgive.

Let's go.

Section One: The Role of Temperament and Understanding in Forgiving

1 Who We Are and What We Do — It matters!

"gnōthi σαυτόν" — "Know thyself"
an inscription on the Oracle of Delphi, often quoted by Plato the Philosopher

Who We Are

Please complete the Adult Temperament Key in Appendix One.

Who are we? That' a question lots of people would like to take a swing at. But we'll forget all the comments from those who don't understand us and treat us as though we are all the same. A maze of advice is out there and can be demotivating if only because it is so confusing. Not so for the ancients. Plato made it clear that "know thyself" was an old established gem of wisdom among the Greeks. Sad that it is regarded in our modern confident age as little needed. Knowing technology, skills, the revelations of Facebook, and the tweets of Twitter seems to be all we need. We could not deceive ourselves more.

Who are we? We are people who are driven by preferences that arise out of our core temperament and its urges — preferences that shape our lives. For example, we may be one of those who feel a real need for social contact or, conversely, love to stay at home with a good book, to be thrill seekers or lovers of science and nature.

Have you stopped to think of what your basic preferences in life are? I'm not talking about a preference for chocolate or a juicy, fragrant steak. I'm referring to preferences to be optimistic and lighthearted or, on the other hand, cautious, concerned, and always in control, to be calm and logical or, on the other hand, warm, emotional and sensitive. These are examples of the preferences that shape our lives and arise out of our temperament's core strengths and urges.

What has temperament to do with forgiving? Much more than you may think. We act out of who we are because that's who we think it best to be. "Listen to your heart" could be better phrased "Listen to the drives of your core temperament because that is your true design and where your lasting happiness lies." Our inner design shapes not only our lives but our thoughts, desires, actions, and non-actions — in other words, the world where our grievances, also, are nursed.

Forgiving is hard for many in the best of times. Are we just trying to make it more complex and all the more difficult by talking about temperament? No, we are making it easier and more effective. Follow your urges where you are strong and do the things that you are naturally empowered to do by your temperament or innerkinetics, as I have termed it, and ease and success will follow in an otherwise difficult struggle.

Preferences
The preferences that are created by our temperament are key, so let's take another look at them. Have you noticed that there are certain patterns in the way you behave? Probably you have realized that you operate with a good deal of consistency around basic preferences. What you prefer become strong drives that you follow most of the time. Another way of looking at it: your basic preferences are not random and don't keep changing with the whim of the moment. You were born with them. They are so second nature to you that it may be a reason why you probably don't know what they are.

14

Think of physical preferences. Take a piece of paper and write anything — your name, for example. Then write it with your non-preferred hand. Without even writing your name with each hand you can imagine the result. You prefer one hand over the other. You have just placed yourself in a group of people or a category called "left-handed" or "right-handed."

Now, think about some of those unseen preferences that reside somewhere inside of you — in your temperament. Call to mind several of your friends or family members and reflect on each of them. Are some more extroverted than the others? Is there one who seems more reserved, introverted, and private — even happy to be on their own? Think deeper about who finds it easier to forgive, the extrovert or introvert? Any ideas about what an extrovert could do to brush away those sad feelings? This and a lot more is what we will be thinking about to help us forgive and find our release from the hurts of others.

Preference Patterns
Basic differences in what we prefer have been studied and noted over millenniums. We have come to understand that the strengths of each temperament form a pattern and, therefore, the preferences that they produce show patterns too.

Let's illustrate that: The SP temperament (the letters S and P refer to one of the four temperaments and are used to avoid giving the temperament a name that is always too restrictive to be very helpful) is a temperament that has the following strengths and is...

Brave, bold, and daring
Spontaneous and impulsive
Effective, tactical, and aggressive
Easily excited
Wants to make an impact

Lighthearted, playful, and tolerant
Ultimate optimist
Action oriented
Focused on the physical senses
Generous
Dramatic in language

Do you notice a pattern? Daring, impulsive, aggressive, easily excited, wants to make an impact, optimistic, dramatic — all the above describe a person who is wanting to drain the last ounce of joy out of each moment and who (in whatever they do) makes an impact, is all about self-expression and thrills, and is designed to do so. This is gregariousness, bravery, and excitement personified.

These strengths seen in the SP are all purposely related. We could even say we would expect them to be found together; they branch out of each other and seem to belong. Each temperament demonstrates the same cohesion.

People of the same temperament can be expected to think, feel, and act in basically the same way in the face of similar challenges. Therefore, in the face of hurt, we can detect the patterns in the way each temperament responds. We can also read what challenges them most and understand how to help them use their strengths to exit the pain and let the past go — in short, how to forgive and move on.

When one person has little trouble in moving on and another is stuck in recrimination and resentment, if we know their temperament, we can understand where each is coming from and what will help each the most. It takes all types to make the world go around and we should respect each person and their difficulties to forgive that are not our own. Learning more in the chapters ahead about the drives that shape and mold us offers some real help in our efforts to forgive.

Temperament is a scientifically validated and well-structured approach to understanding why we think, feel, and act the way we do and how we can find our way out of the mess that anger, resentment, bitterness, and recrimination leave us in. Forgiveness is what we need to do to free ourselves and understanding our temperament will point us to the long lasting and successful restructuring of our freedom and peace of mind as we forgive.

What We Do

We all, in one way or another, respond to what life throws at us. We cannot help but respond. A non-response is also a response. Our responses are seen in what we do — our actions. There's an old proverb that says "actions speak louder than words," and it's often true.

Actions are a form of communication along with emotions, moods, words and, remember, even silence is a communication and an action. Our communication of our response to whatever has happened to us is the first indication of what is going on inside of us. We end up revealing ourselves to the astute observer or listener.

When hurt, we also respond and reveal ourselves. At first the response is an emotion — maybe anger. Then the emotion quickly expresses itself in actions, any of the above actions. Once our actions are out there for others to see, we cannot change them. All we can do is apologize or act differently to signal we have changed our minds or didn't mean what our action showed.

Our First Chance to Change What We Do

After the initial emotion has surged and we have felt it, we can pause right then, evaluate it, and chose to select another emotion — all before we actually act on the initial emotion.

Let's say we haven't acted on our anger yet; we have only felt the surge of anger. It's at this moment we need time to evaluate so we can learn to stifle the emotion while we pause to evaluate it. Is anger the best response, the one we want to give expression to, or is a calm response more appropriate and would it be more effective? When the emotion is mild, we can learn to do this rather easily and train a new neural pathway. "Slow to anger" are the words. Also, slow to speak, which means slow to act. Speech is an action. Learning to pause before we react is going to be key for most temperaments. However, each temperament will do this in its own way.

Our Amazing Virtual World

This chance to change things in the world of our mind before we act on our emotions is where the intelligently emotional person has the first chance to use his analytical mind and select the best action. If he misses the first opportunity to change things, take the next one.

All of our thoughts are like a first draft. Some people always act on the first draft, print and publish it for the world to see, then have to live with what they have done. To change the analogy, they are like the shooter who fires and then thinks about aiming. "Ready, shoot, aim" has very different results from "ready, aim, shoot." Learn to be slower to the trigger. In fact, take careful aim. Think before you act, not after. "Ready, think, act" is intelligent; "ready, act, think" is unintelligent. Our analytical mind wants to be consulted together with our emotions and not be left out of the process or brought in too late. A friend used to always say, "Don't forget to put your mind in gear!"

18

Our Analytical Mind
The analytical mind is slow in comparison to our emotions. Those who act too quickly leave it out of the equation and don't benefit from its attempts at wisdom. We have two minds, as it were — the emotional and the analytical — and both are intelligent. They are meant to act together in unison, helping us choose the best response to all situations.

Unfortunately, if we are of a sensitive and emotional temperament (NF), we have advantages, but when it comes to being slow to anger and slow to speak, we can be a little too trigger happy. This is why we have been given the opportunity to develop the skill of pausing and thinking and, if we don't, we are left with having to apologize because we did not aim before we fired or think before we acted. All temperaments have challenges and this is the NF's Achilles heel.

Practice Pausing
Walk away to think or calm down. If there is no opportunity to withdraw and be alone to think before you act, then learn to adopt a thoughtful expression that silently asks for time. You can also look away, an action you can ingrain into your mental process to remind you to pause.

If you know you are going to face a volatile situation, think of your best response beforehand when you have time to think. Sometimes, if caught without time to think carefully enough,I will use a phrase, like "Let me think," or "I'll think about that." Even those who are not emotionally triggered can still give themselves more time to think. Slow to anger and slow to speak applies to them too. When a "firmer" temperament blurts out their response without care of how it affects others, they will have to change their ready-shoot-aim routine as well.

What We Do Is Who We Become

It is best for all of us to take a hard look at our response routine and improve it for our own good and the good of others. What we typically do creates a default mental pattern for us to follow and we, therefore, follow it most of the time. Create a mental pattern based on "slow to anger and slow to speak" and you will never regret taking the time and the practice to create it.

If our response is anger and we don't get our anger appropriately dealt with, it will morph into resentment and finally into bitterness. That's a bad place to be when trying to forgive.

2 Is this Me or My Nemesis?
(Strengths and Weaknesses)

"Man is born free and everywhere he is in chains"
Jean Jacques Rousseau

We have said at the center of our makeup is our temperament, which contains our strengths, or we could say our core drives and urges that shape who we are and mold our lives.

Strengths and weaknesses — we all have both

We are <u>given</u> our strengths...

- They define us and give us our identity
- They strengthen our belief of who we are
- They show us the direction of our lives
- They create fulfillment
- They make us attractive
- They don't limit us
- They should be our main focus
- They are developed by use

This is good news since we all love to use our strengths and we feel complete and satisfied when we do. But when it comes to forgiving, in particular, you may have noticed that it is not our strengths — rather, our weaknesses — that stop us, make it hard, or trip us up for long periods of time. This is not me; it is my nemesis!

I'm not trying to say we are not responsible and can blame our weaknesses for our not forgiving. Why? Because we create our weaknesses and, therefore, we own them.

We make our weaknesses...one of three ways: we don't use our strengths, overuse them, or misuse them.

- They disempower us
- They lower our self-image
- They weaken our belief system
- They create negative energy
- They create a negative mental environment
- They embitter us
- They rob us of much needed happiness
- They frustrate us
- We then lose the possibility of living to our full potential

From this understanding of strengths and weaknesses some points may be clear to us.

- If all this is true about our strengths and weaknesses, we should focus our lives around our strengths.
- When it comes to forgiving ourselves or others, strengths are where our help comes from and weaknesses are where unforgiveness festers and creates its feelings of ill will.
- We should seek to develop our strengths daily and the positive focus of such a practice will provide the soil for the growth of healthy feelings. Forgiveness thrives in a positive environment and it gives birth to positive emotions.
- We should become acutely aware of the correct use versus the misuse of our strengths.

Before we can help ourselves, live in our strengths, and use them to empower our self-recovery and our ability to forgive, we need to know what our strengths are. Here is a list of the core strengths of each temperament. (For a full discussion of each strength and how to develop them, go to *INNERKINETICS,* by Ray W. Lincoln).

SP Core Strengths
Lives happily in the present moment
Brave, bold, daring
Spontaneous, impulsive
Effective, tactical, aggressive
Easily excited
Wants to make an impact
Lighthearted, playful, tolerant
Ultimate optimist
Action!
A focus on the physical senses, graceful
Generous nature
Dramatic concrete language

SJ Core Strengths
Lives tied to the past
Careful, cautious, concerned
Thoughtful, prepared
Responsible, dependable, solid work ethic
Do what is right, law abiding
Strong need to belong, social, respectable
Steady, not easily shaken
Trusts authority
Supervisors, managers, systems, routines
Stoical
Logistical in work and play
Communicates with the details
Good Samaritan, helpmates
Non-dramatic, concrete speech

NT Core Strengths
Time is related to the task
Strong willed, determined
Strategic, theoretical systems
Intense curiosity
Questioning, skeptical
Independent, self-reliant
Cool, calm, collected
Logical, reasonable, must make sense
Ingenious
Efficient, effective, competent, achieve
Abstract in speech

NF Core Strengths
Lives in and for the future
Idealists, dreamers
Imaginative
Passionate, enthusiastic, value-based decisions
Eager to learn
Trusting
Personal growth, meaning, significance
Sensitive
Intuitive, insightful
Emotional
Empathetic, caring
Humanitarian
Seekers of harmony and haters of discord
Kindhearted
People skills, diplomatic
Real and authentic, ethical
Romantic
Introspective
Perfectionists, must do and be right
Abstract in speech

Note these things about our strengths:

- We may not be aware of all of the strengths in a given temperament as being "in us." That's because not all strengths of that temperament are dominant in each person, but most always are.
- It could also be because we are not as aware of the strengths we don't use often. If we rate the intensity of our strengths, we usually will not rate all of them at the same level of intensity, which indicates we may not see some as typical of us.
- The strengths form a pattern, as we have discussed, and that pattern gives direction and purpose to our lives.
- Any of these strengths, if used positively and effectively, will help us find our way to forgiveness. An SJ, for instance, who is finding it hard to forgive, may find that when they are being a true helpmate, their emotions calm and, together with another strength — thoughtfulness — their use helps them see the hurt in a new light. For an NF, becoming sensitive to another person's stance and not just their own can calm their emotions.
- Strengths are what we are good at and, therefore, they are an easier path for us to follow when we are upset.
- When we are feeling negative, we are not acting according to our strengths. We are acting in our weaknesses and we need to return to focus on the use of our strengths.

Forgiveness becomes impossible when we do not use our strengths as they were designed to be used. Our judgments become unreasonable because of emotional interference and our thinking becomes clouded.

Therefore, in finding ways to make it easier for us to forgive, we will resort, in most cases, to the beneficial use of our strengths. A return to happiness is also a side effect of this method of aiding our ability to forgive.

Section Two: By Temperament — How to Forgive

3 Personalized Solutions for Our Hurts

"Know thyself and thy faults and thus live."
St Augustine

or should he have said

"Know thyself and thy strengths and thus live?"

Earlier we dealt with understanding the role of temperament in forgiving. How each temperament can best handle hurt and enmity is the focus of this section of the book. Solutions for each temperament will be given.

Forgiveness and/or Justice?
This is a question for all of us. All temperaments should read the section on the SJ temperament because SPs will need some of those solutions justly applied at times and NTs and NFs will also benefit, particularly if they have a J in their profile.

Reconciliation, accountability, and justice are not forgiveness but are related activities. At times they cannot be lost sight of, even if we are willing to forgive. Grace, another necessary action in an imperfect society, is by definition "giving someone what they don't deserve" and can be the best (and at times the only) path to forgiveness. This is especially true when insisting on accountability is not an option or when accountability is not, for other reasons, insisted upon. Grace separates personal responsibility from forgiveness and rightly so. Grace and forgiveness are partners that release us from our own damaging responses.

No one would deny that the demand for personal accountability and responsibility are needed in any fair society. Even love must contain goodness and when loving our enemy, goodness and justice are not dismissed. Our legal system is based on justice for a community to survive, so an attempt to find a fair and just solution alongside of our attempts to be willing to forgive can actually aid forgiveness and does so for the SJ in particular.

Let me say this again: forgiveness should not be dependent on justice being performed. If we wait for justice to be enacted before we forgive, we may never be able to forgive. We will be left in the chains of our resentments.

Remember, the goal of forgiveness is to release us from the chains of hurt and the pain of grievance, a goal that at times is achieved quite apart from a just resolution to an infringement. It is the offender's choice or the responsibility of law to pursue or not pursue the path of holding a person responsible and accountable for their actions or non-actions. But if in so doing, forgiveness is not being achieved, the wrong path for release from hurt has been chosen. We must escape the misery of grievances. The path is open because forgiveness is independent of justice.

When to forgive or when not to forgive is not the question. Ask the wrong question and you get the wrong answer. Forgiveness is the only way to find the emancipation that will allow us to move on.

Each temperament must return to its strengths and find there the liberation from the feelings of enmity. So, with strengths in mind, here are some promised solutions for those stuck in their emotional and mental prison of hurts.

4 SP Temperament: Let It Go and Let Live!

Move on!

Because they 'move on' easier and more naturally than others, this strength in the SP, which is the ability to "let it go," needs to be focused on and depended upon by the SP when faced with having to forgive.

> *Whenever they are stuck in enmity, urge them to move on and let it go. SPs understand what letting it go feels like. Give them suggestions of active ways to move on. For example: go work out; take a walk; meet with your friends, and when doing any of these things, enjoy the moment and say nothing about your hurts. Focus on the events of the present and don't reach back into the past and relive it.*

Strange as it sounds, when we have been deeply hurt we want to experience the full extent of our hurt instead of desiring to escape its clutches as soon as possible. Hurt draws us in to feed on its dark emotions. Hurt is negative and the negative environment of the brain does not want to give way to a sunnier positive outlook. Everyone, even the optimistic excitement-seeking SP, may need some extra encouragement to move on and reestablish their sunny optimism if the hurt has been taken very personally.

Simply help them find exciting things to do. "Exciting" means what gives them pleasure or uses their core strengths. Seeking excitement and joy is one of their core strengths. These things must not be things to hope for, but pleasures to be experienced now. Their inner call is to find and enjoy their world in every present moment. Excitement will motivate them to let the hurt go.

Using their analytical brain helps them understand that the loss of pleasure that the hurt is causing is a loss of what they want most and a thorough waste of precious time. Hanging on to misery makes no sense. Help them to make the best of life and reject all that does not live up to this standard. Continuing to feel the pain of past hurts is a condition in the SP that is crying out for help. It is so unlike them.

Because the SP will often feel the need to pay back the one who has hurt or offended them, encourage them not to waste their time on someone whose actions are not deserving. This helps them disconnect from their personalizing of the hurt. Getting even is also a negative world, which is not the healthy world of the SP.

Changing the Picture from Hurt to Opportunity
Here's something else you can do.

> *Paint the mental picture of a person, holding in their hands the key to their chains and a cell door standing wide open while all the guards are busy at some other place. Ask the SP who is wallowing in the hurt why they don't take the key, free themselves, and escape to a life of pleasurable freedom?*

They are all about the freedom of roaming the mountain heights of this life and the thrill of making a positive impact on others. Tell them to get back into the life they have been designed to live. Changing focus for an SP is easily achieved when they become thrill seekers again and seize the opportunity. Forgiveness, as a result, is made easier.

Their adaptability to refocus their lives is a natural use of their strengths and should be used to forgive and move on. Tell them they can always reconnect with an offender when and if they want to, but first, escape to freedom, excitement, and a positive, healthy mind by the road of forgiveness.

Long, instructive dissertations are not their style, so keep all the suggestions short. Action is what they want. An SP will feel the reward of exercising their strengths quicker than, perhaps, any of the temperaments. What you are doing is helping them use their strengths for the motivation they need.

After encouraging them to move on, if the SP is still really stuck in bitterness and personal recrimination, then address their concerns in the same way you would do for an SJ, but do so always with the understanding they must return to optimism. Bitterness breeds emotions that can easily slip into a negative, pessimistic view of things, even for an SP. SJs can be effectively addressed from this point of view. Hence, use some of the motivational skills in the SJ section when pessimism shows itself in an SP. If this does not work, return to an increase in encouraging them to be who they are so capable of being: free souls, who face each moment unchained by the past, whatever pain it holds.

PS: SPs seldom need your help.

34

5 SJ Temperament: The Past Is the Past — Let It Be!

To be read by all temperaments.
The comments under the above section "Forgiveness or Justice" (page 29) are fleshed out here, as well as giving help in rising out of pessimism.

The Value of the Past and the Pit of Pessimism

Because an SJ will typically hold onto the past as long as possible to make sure they have read its lessons and will not forget them, they will be one of the hardest temperaments to free from their hurts. It's also because, when focusing on the hurt, pessimism can take hold of our minds and we make statements like, "My life has been ruined," "The best I have ever had has been destroyed," and "I don't know what I'll do now."   A focus on the past that has developed into a pessimistic attitude is a deep hole to dig out of.

But SJs are no fools and when they decide that this connection with the one who hurt them has no benefit any longer, they will distance the relationship and some can do so without a backwards glance.   They can always consider reestablishing it later if the desire is mutual. For the SJ, in rare cases, severing the relationship can be a helpful move toward forgiveness but alone, still does not free them from the nagging memory. The action is more the action of justice than forgiveness.

When and if the past has no value to the SJ, it will be released. All that remains for them is the decision to forgive, which manifests itself when they let the hurt go or create space and time to get over their enmity. However, for all temperaments, space and time to get over their hurt or sort things out should be limited and have a definite end. Even when needing to pull back and reconstruct our feelings, we should not let hurt and anger live too long in our hearts or it will change us for the worse. "I need space and time and I cannot tell you how much" is a very dangerous pathway to release from our hurts. It is an avoidance of getting on with the decisions of the moment and with life. Forgiveness is a decision first and foremost — firm and irrevocable — and then it is worked out in a process where actions follow the direction of the decision. We rebound from the worst if we aim at rebounding.

Letting go of the past is essential if we want to forgive ourselves. We need to also remember, for all temperaments, forgiving themselves can be the hardest lesson in forgiveness.

There is no exercise more beneficial than mentally forcing ourselves to let go of the past. Why? Because the development of inner strength to discipline and manage our emotions is basic to personal health and happiness.

Grudges
When an SJ is holding a grudge, they are still valuing their connection with the one who hurt them and not yet willing to distance or repair the relationship.

- If they have severed the relationship and moved on, the grudge can be easier to forgive. Severing or distancing the relationship depersonalizes the offense. It's not what we should seek to do first but, as a last resort, can in some circumstances help free us from the chains of hurt. We must, however, carefully count the cost of losing a relationship. Ask: What benefit is the grudge? Ask: What value is the relationship?

- If it is hard to drop the grudge, it is usually because it is hard to drop the relationship. The SJ is loyal and does not go back on their commitments easily. They need also to realize that they have personalized the hurt. An SJ will often have to talk at length with the perceived offender to try to come to a resolution. There's a satisfaction in knowing we have tried. But forgiveness is not about the other person. If all attempts at maintaining the relationship and dismissing the grudge fail, it is a matter of having to do all the things necessary to let the past be the past and applying a mental discipline to release themselves.
- For the SJ, dealing with the issue of being wronged can become more immediately important than freeing themselves from the hurt. But if we don't attempt to free ourselves from the hurt early, it will possess us and this is the SJ's real danger.
- A persistent feeling of ill will can indicate, along with other things, an unwillingness to let the matter drop. Releasing themselves from the ill will then becomes a matter of first making an irrevocable decision to forgive and acting accordingly.
- The Middle English roots for the word "grudge" come from a word meaning to complain, grumble, murmur, and it suggests an important remedy for grudges. Stop talking about them. Sealing up our mouths starves the grudge of the expression it wants. A grudge is hard to hang onto if it is never talked about. This is not internalizing, which is keeping it alive inside our heads by self-talk. It is, instead, starving the grudge.

Feelings of Injustice

Irresponsible or unfair behavior on the part of the offender, for an SJ, should be addressed wherever possible and not circumnavigated. Just asking an SJ to forgive without mention of just and fair actions leaves the SJ with a feeling of incompleteness. SJs want to feel that justice has been addressed if possible. Their sense of responsibility extends not just to themselves but to the maintenance of a fair society. A fair society holds people accountable. Forgiveness and justice have different goals and can work as partners as we have outlined under "Forgiveness or Justice?" in the beginning of this section (page 29).

Most SJs will express their feelings with candor if given the opportunity. But feelings of injustice are not necessarily just if they are the perception of the offended person only. Any of us, not just the SJ, can place full ownership of blame on the other person and not see our own involvement. The freedom and release from hurt that we want is only fully accomplished when we also address the part we might have had in the offense or what led up to the offense. So, for all of us, we need that moment of honesty to assess what has happened and face all the facts.

- Is the injustice truly an injustice? Has the SJ misread the other person's actions or intent?
- Has the SJ also incurred some guilt in how they have behaved as a result of the offense or to cause it? Do they own any responsibility in the matter? If so, owning our responsibility will encourage reconciliation and is an aid to the true release from feelings of unfairness.
- What is their goal for the relationship? Do they want to preserve it, maybe improve it? If so, then urge them to actions of reconciliation that will lead to the achievement of their goal. We do not have to reconcile to forgive but, for the SJ, it offers a rational path to coming to a resolution and dealing with their feelings.
- If the relationship with the one who has offended is harming the SJ or other people, point out the harm and ask them to reevaluate the relationship in the light of the offense. They still may want the relationship, which is fine. If they do, help them to achieve their goal. We can't decide for other people, except in cases where abuse is damaging someone's welfare.

- Justice in the case of relationships is a more complex issue than justice in the face of law.

Revenge or Feelings of Revenge

Revenge can be a major concern for a deeply hurt SJ. SJs are all about fairness, and rightly so, but it is a natural extension to take matters into their own hands. Personal wars result when revenge, even in unrealized ways, is taking place and then enmity has prevailed.

- Someone who needs to forgive but who is bent on revenge cannot have both.
- Forgiveness is best for us.
- Forgiveness offsets the need for revenge.
- Revenge is seldom able to be justified — justice, yes; revenge, no.
- Therefore, for SJs who want a just society, revenge is a blockage on the highway to forgiveness. Also remember, forgiveness is not sweeping the issue under the proverbial rug.

Help an SJ achieve a fair resolution, where appropriate, and also insist on their letting the matter go to drift into the past.

Atoning for the offense

The need to feel the offender should suffer or atone for their "crime" is based in the SJ's firm stance on accountability. That we should be held responsible for our wrong doing is a foundation for any just society but is not necessary for forgiveness.

- We are also back to the fact that we can only control what we can control, and that is seldom the other person — we can only control ourselves. The SJ who wants the offender to suffer more is often fixated in unforgiveness, allowing no chance for resolution or release.

39

- Again, forgiveness is the only path to feeling as though no one has to suffer anymore and all parties have to move on for their own benefits.

Trust

All SJs know relationships are built on trust. Is being able to trust again the reason why they are reticent to forgive?

Consider the following facts:

- We cannot know whether the other person will never let us down again.
- We can never know whether we have enough evidence to trust them again. What about tomorrow? It is unknown. Will they offend again? No conclusive evidence is available to answer that categorically.
- Trusting anyone is a risk. If trusting were not a risk, then we have no need to trust. We can only trust again if we are willing to take a risk again.
- Taking a risk again will come down to how much we value the other person and their contribution to our lives.
- Forgiveness is essential if we are going to take a risk. It is what enables us to take the risk again.

A Stoic Attitude

When SJs have forgiven, you may not notice anything except the restart of relationships again. They may display little remorse or even at times not pause to say sorry. They often do not think it is necessary. In relationships, it is definitely helpful to say sorry, but the essential thing is to resume the relationship with a forgiving attitude. However, if they want to have a satisfying relationship with an NF, saying sorry and sharing a moment of closeness is next door to essential and worth the SJ's effort.

In forgiveness, we don't have to tell the offender we have forgiven them, so this stoical resumption of the relationship can be as genuine an act of forgiveness as an announcement of the forgiveness. Actions that say "I have forgiven you" are the ultimate goal of all true forgiveness.

Do I Have to Admit I Am Wrong?

Admitting wrong when one doesn't feel they are wrong, for an SJ, just simply does not feel right.

Having to admit to themselves that they have been wrong or to face the fact that the act of forgiveness may carry that implication to others is a pill, for some, too hard to swallow. If wrong has not been admitted by the offender, forgiveness can proceed without it, of course. The restoration of the relationship may not. Therefore, help the SJ to keep the following things in mind.

- The truth about forgiveness is that it announces a change of attitude. Without a change of attitude, forgiveness may have been conceived but not given birth.
- Forgiveness says, "Whatever the facts or perceived facts, someone has moved on without further animosity in the matter."
- Forgiveness not only says I have let go of my ill feelings but I have also let go of any claim to revenge.
- Do we have to forgive? No. We can launch a lawsuit, spread harm and hurt, or demand that the offender face his day before his judge. But eventually, we will have to forgive if we want to walk free from the chains of grievance.
- Admitting wrong, even to ourselves, when it is not clear that we have done wrong, does no harm and maybe, good.
- Saying sorry, even when we are not sure we are to blame or even when we are to blame, can be the best of actions. One should be truly sorry for any harm, wittingly or

41

unwittingly, with intent or without intent, in reality or only in faulty perception, caused another person. And one can be sorry in this way without admitting blame. All a sensitive NF wants is not so much the admission of blame but the harmony of a moment of shared and voiced concern for each other.

- If admitting wrong is so hard to do, is pride an issue?
- Always act in the interests of your highest values. Ask, "What is my highest value that I want to preserve?"

6 NT Temperament: Do We Have to Understand?

Independence marks the NT. Typically, they don't want to be beholden to anyone. They certainly don't want to be under another's control. The NT believes we should be able to take care of ourselves and they want to raise self-reliant children too. Self-reliance does not readily see the need of forgiveness or of restoring relationships that have proved to be tenuous.

Add to this that the NT is not typically as emotionally impacted by the hurts of others as the other temperaments. It is easier for them to not pay attention to hurts because hurts, if focused on, can activate unwanted emotional traumas that they want to avoid. So, what's the big deal about hurts? Just don't think about them or about the person who has inflicted them. Keep moving on in the direction of your interests and tasks. The NT's mind is too busy to be worried with hurts, unless they begin to invade the NT's busy mind. There is too much to explore and think about than such insignificant moments.

Not all NTs think in such absolute terms. Some value emotion and are not dramatically independent either, but if either of these perspectives lessen the need for forgiveness, the NT's beliefs need some adjustment in order to be able to experience the cleansing of forgiveness.

We start with the NTs who wonder if there is such a need for forgiveness. They handle their grievances and ills with reaffirmed independence and by creating a cool distance that keeps their offenders at bay and does not stir their own emotions.

However, these NTs are just kidding themselves. They seek companionship and the warmth of approval, although not with the passion of the other temperaments. They want friendships that make sense and if they don't, the friendship is not entertained in the first place. Can an NT be hurt? Yes! However, the emotions are hidden as quickly as they show themselves in most cases. Signs of a mild disturbance is the level of their typical show of emotionality. If hurt deeply, it is hidden until they have settled on the best action to take or, uncharacteristically, they might explode in anger and then move on.

They also seek clear minds and a mind full of ill will is not free of the clutter of hurt and cannot operate as efficiently. To be an NT is to take care of your mind. Forgiveness does just that for the embittered NT.

Hurt Requires a Strategy
An NT lives a strategized life. Any hurt is a contingency they have to deal with. Sometimes the NT does not create a strategy for their relationships. This typically happens when their focus is strongly elsewhere and their emotions are calm and protected. A hurt can then catch them by surprise.

When they do create a strategy for their relationships, they plan to deal with common contingencies and follow their plan. Their plan may look like this: disregard the hurt if at all possible, consider removing oneself from the scene of disturbance, and focus on the current task. If confrontation is necessary, state your case with confidence and walk away; keep the attacker at a distance with the skillful use of cool silence.

This may work at first, but soon resentment builds in both parties and the issue becomes a deep divide between them. At worst they walk away from the relationship and move on with a lack of effective forgiveness that got them into the problem in the first place. Therefore, for the NT, forgiveness is a necessary part of any relationship strategy. Convince them of its benefits.

Logic and Reason

All actions and plans must be reasonable to the NT. "What is the most rational thing to do?" they ask themselves. Mostly, the answers they find are not only logical but pragmatic. The NT can walk the path of reason easily and refuse to walk any other path. Emotion is seen as having little or no reason, so if to forgive can be seen as reasonable and makes sense to them, they will readily forgive and move on quickly.

Their moving on can seem too cool for the emotionally rich NFs. The issues that enable them to forgive, for NTs and NFs, are opposites — reason and emotional connection. Logic and emotion are both mind functions. The NTs will be helped more by using reason than the presence of good and warm emotions.

Reaction to "Un-forgivable" Hurt

If the hurt seems un-forgivable, NTs seek to withdraw and wall themselves off from their hurt emotions. But suppressed emotions do not go away simply because they are held down. Ignoring them or refusing to listen to them takes its unhealthy toll on all of us. These unresolved emotions will shape the kind of life we will be forced to live. Forgiveness resolves our emotional concerns. All temperaments need to understand the practical profundity of that statement.

Our attitudes and even our effectiveness are controlled by our hurts as well as our successes. A strong case can be made for the unreasonableness of ignoring the emotions of hurt and trying to stuff a grievance. Separating from the offender does not always make sense either. Only forgiveness cleans the human heart.

45

Is Reason Adequate to Remake Our Emotions?

The use of rationality and logic are helpful but not adequate tools to deal with the tangled knots of life, which are mostly emotional in nature. What a tangled mess hurt emotions weave!

When the NT can be convinced to view emotions as facts of life, and as equally important pieces of evidence for logic to wrestle with, a resolution is in sight. Without emotions being viewed as facts, the picture is incomplete, of course, and the NT is making decisions that are not based on all the facts.

Even for the NT, forgiveness has more to do with settling the score with their emotions than with their reason. The feelings, more than the facts of the happening that created the hurt, must be reconciled. Regardless of how they feel about it, NTs are not devoid of emotion. Forgiveness is an act of our emotions as well as our rational mind, and only if both are adequately satisfied will the forgiveness be real.

Again, emotion is a response to what has happened to us, and how reason can be understood as adequate on its own to resolve enmity seems broken logic. Emotion is always, and always will be, involved along with reason in healing.

The issue for the NT is often how to handle emotion and what to do with it if I can grasp it? The answer for the NT is:

- First, identify the emotion that is hindering a willingness to forgive
- Recognize its negative impact on your life
- Determine to replace it with a healthy emotion that makes sense to you
- Cease to talk or think in terms of the negative emotion
- Construct a plan to re-engage with your strengths and focus on using them. Get back to the business of being who you are.

Only then can the NT grasp and replace the offending emotions, which in the first place were their own response to the situation.

Skepticism and Suspicion

Further troubles await the NT who is struggling with forgiveness. Skepticism, a natural core strength that belongs in their temperament, can be easily misused or overused, creating a roadblock on the way to freedom from their grievances.

Also for the NT, suspicion arising from a negative use of their skepticism can be especially hard to eradicate. The nature of rationality is not to ignore the facts and not to be fooled by them. Suspicion that there is an ulterior motive behind the action or that the intent is not honorable can, therefore, become a mental road block to the willingness to forgive.

If an NT feels that he may be hurt again by the same person, he will plan a way around what that person may do to him and forgiveness is not usually in that plan. Ever skeptical and strategically prepared is their compass for life.

How can they forgive when they are suspicious of more hurt? The problem is expressed in the question of the disciple Peter: "How many times should I forgive? Seven times?" The answer, no doubt, stunned him: "seventy times seven," which requires bookkeeping most of us do not have the patience for. And if we don't keep count (the meaning of the reply is to show the false nature of keeping count when forgiving), we will need to drop our suspicion and run the risk of forgiveness, which opens a new page and starts life again with a clean heart. Forgiveness is the high road, but also the beginning of a new road each time.

- Skepticism comes in two forms: positive, which is an invaluable tool for discovery, and negative, which can become a life of wary suspicion and debilitating doubt.
- The NT must experience feeling free from negative skepticism in order to forgive. The negative use of a positive strength has to be let go.
- To aid in forgiveness, the NT can also appreciate the logic of living a life that is not hampered and clouded by the hurts others have committed. They can only be really independent when they are independent of the hurts of others and the grievances that grip their minds.
- Consider also, suspicion holds us back from the future because it makes us fearful to enter the future. Forgiveness makes us face an unknown future and a relationship is always an adventure with the unknown.
- Forgiveness is releasing the past, letting the future be what it may with the confidence that we will be able to negotiate our way successfully, while also letting the present be what it is. Negative skepticism will not let us do that.
- To live happily and effectively between the ups and downs of the past and the fears of an unknown future is achieved with the skill of selecting intelligent emotions — being intelligently emotional, in other words. Intelligent emotions are those that allow us to face the future without fear and a suspicious skepticism.
- Part of their thinking and planning can consider ways to overcome any effect the hurt may have had on themselves. This is strategy to live above and beyond hurt and be impregnable or indestructible to their enemy. When the NT thinks this way, letting the hurt go can make sense to them.

Having to Understand
Once again, we encounter the problem of having to understand before we can forgive. An NT is all about their mind and when they cannot understand why something has

happened, they don't want to move on until they do understand. "Why" is a big word for them. When "why" can't be answered, it creates another mental block.

But as we have already said:

- We will never be in possession of all the facts. Subjective motivations and hidden schemes can be undiscoverable. Besides, we are limited creatures with limited knowledge and limited ability to see all that there is to see.
- When a person does wrong, it is usually not reasonable, so how can we understand how it makes sense when it is an unreasonable act?
- If we did understand, an unreasonable act would still make no sense to us.
- To let a lack of understanding stop us from forgiving makes no sense. Is there anything that is more important than getting past the hurt and back to a life that is free from the chains of the past?

Values
All of us have created our own set of beliefs, which reflect our values. Our values can often be false because we adopt most of them from others and our culture without thinking about them deeply. Therefore, the desire to forgive can be wrecked on the rocks of unhealthy or unhelpful values. The NT, in order to be free to forgive, may need to reconsider their values.

When we can't see beyond the hurt, our true values can also be obscured. For example, when the value of revenge is greater than the value of our personal freedom from ill feelings, we are checking ourselves into an emotional prison. Forgiveness is then devalued.

For the NT, the power and accuracy of logical thinking is conditioned by the selection and priorities of our values. A

49

false presupposition or assumption about our true needs can topple the best of logical structures. Peace of mind, achieved by forgiveness and harmony in our relationships, is a priority for the effective thinker to grant great value to.

7 NF Temperament: Intelligent Emotions Are the Key.

NFs face their biggest challenge when they consider forgiveness: emotions! It's not just emotions but their natural reaction to hurt emotions: namely self-defense by means of withdrawal or, conversely, the explosive appearance of anger. They instinctively know that self-management of their emotions is a thing they must learn if they want to be successful in life and relationships.

An NF is designed with a number of strengths that need to be addressed to make forgiveness possible. These strengths must be used beneficially, not detrimentally.

Why is it that they seem to have such a problem with keeping their emotions in check? There are several things.

- First, when we are hurt by what people have said or done or not said or done, anger is an automatic result. It was back in 1958 that Strecker and Appel, two psychologists, wrote (to some people's surprise) in *Discovering Ourselves* that hurt and anger always seem to appear together.
- Emotions flare when we are hurt and if we judge the intent of the offender as an attempt to hurt us, we instantly find ourselves angry at the assailant.
- The anger of an NF rises quickly and forcefully because they are very sensitive to any and all hurts.
- Other people do the same, but they seem to have effective ways to disarm the hurt or lessen it, such as shrugging it off or not thinking it worthy of their reaction. Not so for the NF.

NFs can be overwhelmed by hurt. When our emotions go on automatic, we can't be blamed for them. We can't excuse ourselves altogether for the explosion either. We must own whatever response we end up with after selecting an appropriate emotion or failing to do so. We also have a chance and an ability to change our emotions. The sensitive NF has to react responsibly, regardless of how hard it is. The way we are made must never be used as an excuse for our behavior. If it is used as an excuse, ultimately, everything can be excused.

If changing the emotion from anger to a calmer rational approach is effectively achieved, the hurt still remains and needs the ointment of forgiveness to heal. What does an NF do about the hurt? If the NF doesn't do something quickly, it can soon morph into more harmful emotions: the feelings of resentment, bitterness, and rejection of the offender. This is where forgiveness comes into the game of life. For the NF, the quicker they seek and find a forgiving spirit and an understanding stance, the more likely they are to corral the hurt and keep it from exploding into those bitter emotions that make forgiveness so difficult for them.

Therefore, they should be encouraged to walk away or in any effective way calm their emotions as soon as possible and engage their analytical mind. It's when reason takes over that the emotions can most effectively be reined in and changed.

Reason
For the emotional NF, reason is a gift from God to be exercised and trained for battle on the field of personal hurt.

To be reasonable is the desire of the NF. Their sense of integrity insists on it. They must be fair. Plato called them "noetic," meaning the temperament with understanding, insight, perception, and as Plato detected, they also exhibit a love of reason and mind.

But if their emotions are constantly stirred with continued accusations and criticisms, they will not easily resort to reason, believing the judgments of their emotions to be correct. This will send them into a defensive mode. How do we help them or how do they help themselves?

- Start by trying to understand and empathize with the offender. It should be the first mental exercise for NFs when hurt. They must try, even if they can't understand.
- It is a love of the NF to empathize, and resorting to an understanding mode certainly can be attractive to them.
- If very deeply hurt, they need time alone to reflect and gather themselves for the emotional battle ahead. They can gather themselves best by focusing on the solutions to the problem that they can implement and over which they have control. Help in determining whether their solutions are helpful or not should be sought.
- Nursing their hurt is the beginning of being taken captive by their emotions, so this is a no-no.
- If they let their emotions win the early battle for their mind, it is going to be all the harder for them to come to reasonableness and forgiveness. Hard or not, the sooner the NF wins the battle for their minds and creates a positive mind, the sooner they will save themselves from days, and perhaps months, of pain and anger. Forgiveness creates a positive mind.
- Reason makes sense to the NF whose emotions have not negatively escalated or have already calmed. Calming the emotions is paramount to forgiving and the use of reason will help them forgive.
- It's not "first, can I find a rationale for why the hurt was delivered against me in the first place?" It is "what is my reasonable path that does not deny my emotions but becomes selective of which are the best, helpful, and positive emotions for me to nurture?"
- Negative emotions thrive and escalate in a negative mind.

- Reason with an NF when they are calm and they will usually be easily persuaded to consider the option of forgiveness.

Harmony

To forgive brings the best of feelings and a return to harmony, which NFs crave. When harmony has been disturbed and emotions hurt, the hurt must be healed by forgiveness before the harmony can be realistically restored. How are emotions healed?

Hurt emotions are inflamed feelings and need anti-inflammatory treatment before they can begin to heal.

- Provide time to think and calm voices. Even a glimpse of love in the midst of an attempt to work things out can start the healing.
- The return of love is, of course, magic.
- The more gently you approach their wounded emotions, the more likely the NF will welcome your approaches.
- They will seldom be ready to quickly accept the approaches of the one who has hurt them.

Passion

Passion is exhibited over what they see as an injustice. It is a negative passion usually expressed in anger. They think not so much in terms of justifying their passion as making a stand for what they perceive as the right. Therefore, they can get stuck on what they see as a lack of integrity and they hammer away at what, in their perception, is right.

It may be an issue of integrity, but being right when hurt is no advance toward positive healthy emotions for the NF.

NFs need to see that there is more than one issue at hand:

1. The issue over an injustice, which is stirring their passion.
2. The issue of their rising resentment, bitterness, and anger that is causing them harm.
3. The issue of the image they are projecting and the conflict they are engendering.
4. And, probably, the issue of being blind to other ways of handling the injustice.

Issues need to be prioritized when passion is hot. Passion focuses on the wrong and does not scan for alternative pathways. Passion narrows rather than broadens our vision.

- The NF must deal with their own anger first, which means calming the emotion and then making a search for a solution to the injustice if that is possible.
- Second, working through the issue in a calm and reasonable manner to come to the best just resolution possible helps calm their passion.
- Resolutions are not always possible. Acceptance of such situations is then the healthy alternative that will lead them to forgiveness.
- Forgiveness requires acceptance but does not insist on restoring the relationship. That is the offended's choice.

Having to Understand
Like others, they can get stuck on having to understand. Humans do not like to proceed when their security or safety ahead is unknown. The unknown scares us. The NF lives happily only when they have hope, and a lack of knowledge about what might happen can destroy hope. If I don't understand why and with what intention the person did what they did, how can I know I will not be made a fool if I forgive? Remember, forgiveness is not about restoring relationships, although that may be your goal. It is about finding release

from the hurt. We often get stuck on a false understanding of what forgiveness is.

Finding Trust Again

Because they are trusting of people, when hurt, the NFs feel that they have trusted the offender and their trust has been abused. This may be so, but if a resolution is to be found, they will have to trust again. The trust can be conditional on agreed behavior, but trust they must. No NF can exist in a relationship without feeling that they are safe to trust. Trust is peace and harmony and for an NF, harmony is essential in all meaningful relationships.

This is another example of confusing forgiveness, in this case, with the urge to restore trust or with the inability to trust. If the NF would separate the issues that surround forgiveness from forgiveness, they would be able to forgive much easier.

Someone Must Suffer

The feeling that someone has to suffer with them is a variation of their felt need for justice. But the NF is led astray if they think that someone suffering like they are suffering will assuage their hurt or make forgiveness easier. It can also make them feel the uneasiness that they may be guilty of hurting others too.

They will soon be sorry for any hurt they may have inflicted and they would rather take the blame if harmony can be restored. However, remember the only harmony forgiveness is about is our inner harmony. Harmony in a broken relationship requires restoration. Find inner harmony, and that can be done in short order when we forgive.

Self-Worth

When blame enters the NF's mind, it is a passionate blaming of people or circumstances to preserve whatever feelings of self-worth the NF has left. (NFs typically have low self-images).

Keeping self-worth high is an essential struggle for an ultra-introspective being. Consider:

- There is no purpose, meaning, or reason for life if we have no sense of worth, and the NF feels this poignantly.
- Whenever they feel their self-worth slipping away, they react instantly.
- That fear of a loss of self-worth sparks the emotion to blame because it diverts the nagging fear that they are once again failures at life. If it is someone else that is to blame, then it is not me that has digressed and I can defend my worth. This is often why they blame.
- When they must finally see for themselves that they were at least in part to blame, they must deal with the blow to their self-image, and this is where they can crumble into a self-induced depression because they feel as though they are no good. It's not that they want to feel depressed either!

There is only one real beneficial resolution to the whole issue of blame, and that is forgiveness because it cleans the NF's slate and makes them feel white, like snow, again — at least until the next time they fail.

Life, for the NF, is a continual forgiving of themselves and of any hurts they have imposed on others in the struggle to live a meaningful life of personal integrity. When the emphasis of their temperament is on a critical self-introspection, the restoration of personal integrity is of utmost importance or the NF will slump into depression.

Self-worth is threatened even more by the loss of a friendship and the feelings of guilt for what they have to own as their own failures. An NF can forgive readily when they have a reasonably healthy self-image.

Self-image is what we think about ourselves and the NF must face their sad attempt, at times, to bring someone down so that they can feel better about themselves. The solution to self-image is not a struggle to feel proud of oneself but a feeling that we are important to this world and we have a clean slate. Looking back over their shoulder to their failures is misery for the NF. Forgiveness means, for them, looking back and not seeing a trail of failures in their wake but a life that renews itself and gets better with the struggle.

Hyper Sensitivity

The hurt an NF feels is often accompanied by an attempt at self-defense due to their being hypersensitive to the inner pain of constantly, in their perceptions, being wounded. They are hypersensitive to the hurt they feel when someone attacks their integrity or self-image as well as when the attack is on someone else's self-worth. It can be something someone has said or done or not said or done. An oversensitive NF can be too easily hurt. All NFs, though, are hurt frequently because they have no acceptable mechanism to ward off the hurts. Sensitivity senses more hurts than non-sensitivity.

- Oversensitive and hypersensitive are not the same thing. *Hyper* means "very" and *over* means "too much."
- It is hard for others to value this much needed hypersensitivity that produces such things as a healing empathy and truly loving sacrifice. NFs bring to the world a sensitivity that also sees beauty in all things good and lifts emotion to its highest expressions.
- In hypersensitivity, great giftedness can be found. This potential for sensitivity, resulting in giftedness, is seen in

all artistic geniuses, although in NFs, it is not limited to the arts.
- NFs defend themselves fiercely when hurt. It is either expressed in an outward (usually verbal) attack on the offender or a withdrawal, which can be frigid, to avoid all further hurt.
- When the emotions are calmed, the NF can usually admit to being oversensitive if the other person will admit to having hurt them and show some sign of sorrow. When that doesn't happen, the NF needs time to calm and heal the hurt.
- Strong emotions do not recede with haste. The greater the sensitivity, the stronger the currents of hurt.
- Without forgiveness, this healing is not wholesome and carries the bitterness of the past with it.
- Sometimes they hate their hypersensitive nature and yet, it is what makes them so empathetic, romantic, emotional, and kind. A fresh use of these strengths will calm their emotions most effectively and quickly.
- If mad with anger, the need to suddenly be kind and offer assistance to someone else will force a change of emotions, and that means the anger abates and forgiveness is seriously contemplated.
- There is no lasting resolution to hurt aside from a spirit of forgiveness, in which the NF heals and finds acceptance and love again.

To summarize the benefits of forgiveness, it:
- Restores harmony and paves the way for love to flow fresh and clean again
- Brings calm to agitated emotions
- Restores and heals friendships
- Allows the NF to move on to hope again
- Develops their typical loving nature
- Frees them from emotions that demotivate them.

Hope
Because effectively putting the hurt behind them is necessary for an NF, we can see the essential nature of hope for them.

- An NF is oriented toward the future, searching in hope for its opportunities. To live without hope is an NF's ultimate misery. Therefore, helping them to find hope is sometimes all they need in order to be willing to forgive. Hope is found in putting hurts far, far behind.
- Putting hurts far behind and letting them go cannot occur, for the NF, without being freed from their ill feelings. Once again, for the NF, forgiveness is about coming to terms with their feelings.
- Show them the hope that forgiveness brings to a renewal of relationship, for example, and they are nearer to forgiving.
- Remind them that harmony lies the other side of a firm decision to forgive that is followed by immediate actions toward forgiveness.
- Help them find hope in their future and they will forgive more readily and move on.
- An NF really wants to forget at least enough to effectively put it out of their mind. To put the grievance out of their mind is accomplished by filling their mind with love and harmony and pleasant feelings. When these feelings are found, the NF is resistant to looking back at the pain.
- Forgiveness is the result of rewriting their minds and thoughts positively. They can begin this the moment desire lifts its head and signals "Go."

Intuition
NFs are full of insights into what the other person is feeling, and this can delay and inhibit the decision to forgive if the insights are mistaken or not helpful.

- If they intuit continued hurt, they will react quickly for self-protection.

60

- If they sense falseness or harmful intent in another person's actions or feelings, then it becomes a fact on which they act, again in self-defense.
- When hurt, they seldom intuit any good intent in the other person. The lines of intuitive communication are too disrupted by the static of hurt.

These are situations where their intuition can damage them and make it difficult for them to see hope and a light at the end of the tunnel.

Idealism
"How the mighty have fallen." To the NF, when anyone who they have idealized has shown less than the NF's expectations, oh how the mighty have fallen!

- Forgiveness of this kind requires building renewed expectations, setting the loved one back on the pedestal after a heart-felt forgiveness and an attempt at admiring them again.
- NFs are idealists rather than realists. They justify this stance by pointing out that one should never establish an aim that is less than ideal. In fact, perfection makes sense to them as the target of all their feelings and aspirations. To try to make them realists is not the most productive way to help them to forgiveness, rather...
- Focus them on the good points of their fallen offender and when they do see again the good points, forgiveness is a forethought and before you know it, an afterthought.

Personalizing Hurts
NFs, along with some others from the other temperaments, maximize their hurts by personalizing them. For all who suffer from personalizing the hurt here are some thoughts...

- Some hurts and deliberate attacks are meant to be accepted as personal. In forgiveness, we are not asked to be unconcerned about intent, nor does it stop us releasing ourselves from the hurt of the offense.
- When we take the offense personally, however, we increase the difficulty of forgiving the offender.
- Personal or not, forgiveness is the only route to freedom from being hurt *ad infinitum*.
- How does personalizing the hurt make it so hard to forgive? By making it all about the most tender of an NF's emotions, the personal feelings.
- A personal hurt that is forgiven is not necessarily excused and we may decide to forgive, but not restore the relationship. That is our choice, as is the consequences of our choice.

Forgiveness must be seen as an act that lets the grievance drift downstream, out of sight, and out of the reach of continuing personal harm and pain. Forgiveness actually depersonalizes the hurt.

Conclusion

The task of forgiveness is made easier by an understanding of temperament — our innerkinetics. Therefore, it is helpful to summarize the main principles we have emphasized in this book. Assuming you have completed the Temperament Key and identified your temperament, the following is a handy checklist to tell you if you are on track to healing and health of mind and soul.

- We are not all the same and we don't have the same difficulties with having to forgive. "Please understand me" is the cry from all of us. Pay attention to your temperament.
- Understanding how we function is important to our being able to act in the healthiest way. (See the section on "What We Do").
- Please don't focus on your weaknesses and your struggles. If you do, you will increase the difficulty you are having with forgiveness.
- Focus on the use and the building of your strengths and you will begin to feel the freedom of a positive world — the only world where healing is found. Healing is never found in a negative mental or emotional world.
- Each temperament is a cohesive world that wants to function and feel its fulfillment. Healing is all about feeling that fulfillment and personal health again. Place the emphasis of all your healing efforts and wishes on being who you are in your strengths and who you are designed to be. Then you can move on and up, releasing the chains of hurt for better things.
- Pay attention to your temperament's struggles only in order to focus on its strengths. Remember, healing is all

about applying the ointment, not digging around in the wound, ever searching for some more emotional contaminants. There are many self-healing life forces built into us and we benefit from them when we function like we are designed to function.

Move on, look up — not back — and find your path to your highest potential.

The Temperament Key

The Adult Temperament Key used here has been developed using the principles of research into temperament that Myers-Briggs, Keirsey, Harkey-Jourgensen, and others have used for the development of their assessments. These principles, when used in assessments, have proven very reliable and can be depended upon. Any of the above named assessments of temperament are excellent guides to the discovery of how we are made on the inside.

As long as you carefully follow the instructions for the Adult Temperament Key presented here, you should get excellent results.

This is a very positive assessment. We are looking for your strengths, not your weaknesses. There are no wrong answers since it is a self-evaluation. However, be as accurate as possible. Read these instructions carefully since a knowledgeable guide is not looking over your shoulder and you can't ask for help. It is imperative that you answer according to these instructions.

- *Answer these questions according to your preferences (what you prefer), not according to what you think others would have you become.*
- *Answer each question individually. Don't try to be consistent.*
- *Aim to get through the key in about 20 minutes or less.*
- *Think carefully about each answer, but avoid over-thinking, which can lead to confusion. If you are over-thinking, ask yourself "What am I the most?"*
- *Again, let me put it this way: You will see yourself as both (a) and (b) in some of the questions. Your answer should be what you see yourself to be the most, or what you prefer the most or makes you feel most comfortable.*
- *Your preferences are often different at home than at work. This can be because, at work certain things are required of you and, therefore, they have become your work preferences. You prefer to do it that way at work since that's what is good for you. If your work preferences differ from your home preferences, answer according to your home preferences.*
- *We want to know what really beats in your breast, what really satisfies, fulfills, or pleases you the most.*

The results should be accurate but if you attend one of my seminars, ask to be checked again. It's a service we provide. When you read the descriptions of the temperaments in chapters seven, eight, nine, and ten, you will determine whether they match your results in the temperament key. If they do not match the descriptions, then you answered with something else in mind and you will need to confirm the temperament most like you.

This check on your answers is very helpful. The ones who are most likely to be confused about themselves are the NFs. They are the complicated temperament and have the greatest difficulties in understanding themselves for that understandable reason. Now, proceed with careful thought.

<u>Note:</u> You may also go to our website at <u>www.raywlincoln.com</u>/ RESOURCES where you will find a free, downloadable Adult Temperament Key.

ADULT TEMPERAMENT KEY

Check (A) or (B) for each question. Please answer ALL questions.

1. *At social gatherings do you prefer to*
   _____ *A. Socialize with everyone*
   _____ *B. Stick to your friends*

2. *Are you more in touch with*
   _____ *A. The real world*
   _____ *B. The world inside your mind; the world of possibilities*

3. *Do you rely more on, or take more notice of*
   _____ *A. Your experiences*
   _____ *B. Your hunches or gut feelings*

4. *Are you (most of the time)*
   _____ *A. Cool, calm, and collected*
   _____ *B. Friendly and warm*

5. *When evaluating people do you tend to be*
   _____ *A. Impersonal and frank*
   _____ *B. Personal and considerate*

6. *Do you mostly feel a sense of*
   _____ *A. Urgency/upset if you are not on time*
   _____ *B. Relaxed about time.*

7. *When you see a mess do you*
   _____ *A. Have an urge to tidy it up*
   _____ *B. Feel reasonably comfortable living with it*

8. *Would you describe yourself as*
   _____ *A. Outgoing/demonstrative/easy to approach*
   _____ *B. Somewhat reserved/private*

9. *Which are you best at*
   _____ *A. Focusing on details*
   _____ *B. Catching the big picture, the connections, the patterns*

67

10. Children should be
_____ A. Made to be more responsible
_____ B. Encouraged to exercise their imagination and make-believe more

11. When making decisions, are you more influenced by
_____ A. The facts or impersonal data
_____ B. Personal feelings

12. Do you feel more yourself when giving
_____ A. Honest criticism
_____ B. Support, approval, and encouragement

13. Do you work best
_____ A. Scheduled; to deadlines
_____ B. Unscheduled; no deadlines

14. For a vacation do you prefer to
_____ A. Plan ahead of time
_____ B. Choose as you go

15. When you are with others do you usually
_____ A. Initiate the conversation
_____ B. Listen and tend to be slow to speak

16. Most of the time, facts
_____ A. Should be taken at face value.
_____ B. Suggest ideas, possibilities, or principles.

17. Do you mostly feel
_____ A. In touch with the real world
_____ B. Somewhat removed, lost in thought

18. When in an argument or discussion do you care more about
_____ A. Defending your position and being right
_____ B. Finding harmony and agreement

19. With others do you tend to be
_____ A. Firm
_____ B. Gentle

20. Do you see yourself as
_____ A. Predictable
_____ B. Unpredictable

21. Do you mostly prefer to
_____ A. Get things done; come to closure
_____ B. Explore alternatives; keep options open

22. After two hours at a party are you
_____ A. More energized than when you arrived
_____ B. Losing your energy

23. Which best describes you
_____ A. Down to earth, practical
_____ B. Imaginative, an idea person

24. Which do you finally rely on more
_____ A. Common sense
_____ B. Your intuition/insights or your own analysis

25. In other people, which appeals to you most
_____ A. A strong will
_____ B. Warm emotions

26. Are you more controlled by
_____ A. Your head/thought
_____ B. Your heart/emotions

27. Are you typically
_____ A. Eager to get decisions made
_____ B. Not keen on making decisions

28. On the whole do you spend your money
_____ A. Cautiously
_____ B. Impulsively

29. When you have lost energy, do you find yourself mostly
_____ A. Seeking out people
_____ B. Seeking out solitude/a quiet corner

30. Do dreamers
_____ A. Annoy you somewhat
_____ B. Fascinate and interest you

31. Do you rely more
_____ A. On your five senses
_____ B. On your sixth sense/intuition

32. Are you more
_____ A. Tough-minded
_____ B. Tenderhearted

33. Would you more likely choose to be
_____ A. Truthful
_____ B. Tactful

34. Do you see yourself as more
_____ A. Serious and determined
_____ B. Relaxed and easygoing

35. Do you feel more comfortable when
_____ A. Things are decided
_____ B. Your options are still open

36. Would you say you mostly
_____ A. Show your feelings readily
_____ B. Are private about your feelings and keep them inside

37. Would you prefer
_____ A. To be in touch with reality
_____ B. To exercise a creative imagination

38. Is your way of thinking more
_____ A. Conventional
_____ B. Original and creative

39. What motivates you more
_____ A. Solid evidence
_____ B. An emotional appeal

40. Would you rather be known for
_____ A. Being a consistent thinker
_____ B. Having harmonious relationships

41. Do you tend to
_____ A. Value routines
_____ B. Dislike routines

42. Do you live more with
_____ A. A little sense of urgency
_____ B. A leisurely pace

43. Do you have
_____ A. Many friends and count them all your close friends
_____ B. Few friends, and only one or two that are deep friends

44. Do you place more emphasis on what you see
_____ A. With your physical eyes
_____ B. With your mind's eye

45. Are you
_____ A. Thick skinned; not hurt easily
_____ B. Thin skinned; hurt easily

46. When you are asked to create a "To Do" list, does it
_____ A. Seem like the right thing to do and do you feel it will be helpful
_____ B. Bug you and seem more like an unnecessary chore

47. Which word attracts you most or describes you best?
_____ A. Talkative
_____ B. Quiet

48. Which words attract you most or describe you best?
_____ A. Present realities
_____ B. Future hopes

49. Which word(s) attracts you most or describe(s) you best?
_____ A. Logic
_____ B. Loving heart

50. *Which word attracts you most or describes you best?*
_____ A. Plan
_____ B. Impulse

51. *Which word attracts you most or describes you best?*
_____ A. Party
_____ B. Home

52. *Which word(s) attracts you most or describe(s) you best?*
_____ A. Common sense
_____ B. Vision

53. *Which word attracts you most or describes you best?*
_____ A. Justice
_____ B. Mercy

54. *Which word attracts you most or describes you best?*
_____ A. Concerned
_____ B. Carefree

SCORE SHEET

Instructions for the score sheet:
1. *Place a* ☒ *in the appropriate column (A or B) to indicate the answer you chose for each numbered question. [Please note that the numbers run from left to right across the chart.]*
2. *Count the number of "As" in column #1 and write that number in box "c," above the "E." Count the number of "Bs" in column #1 and write that number in box "d," above the I.*
3. *Count the number of "As" in column #2 and write that number in box "e." Count the number of "Bs" in column #2 and write that number in box "f."*
4. *Count the number of "As" in column #3 and write that number box "g." Count the number of "Bs" in column #3 and write that number in box "h."*
5. *Add the number of "As" for columns 2 and 3 together and write the total in box "i." Add the number of "Bs" for columns 2 and 3 and write that number in box "j."*
6. *Repeat the steps in instructions 2-5 above for columns 4/5 and 6/7.*
7. *Which did you have more of, "Es" or "Is"? _____*
Which did you have more of, "Ss" or "Ns"? _____

72

Which did you have more of, "Ts" or "Fs"? _____
Which did you have more of, "Js" or "Ps"? _____

8. *In the four letters you listed in Instruction #7, which two-letter combination below is present? Circle it!*

S and P   *S and J*   *N and T*   *N and F*

	1			2			3			4			5			6			7	
	A	**B**		**A**	**B**		**A**	**B**		**A**	**B**		**A**	**B**		**A**	**B**		**A**	**B**
1			2			3			4			5			6			7		
8			9			10			11			12			13			14		
15			16			17			18			19			20			21		
22			23			24			25			26			27			28		
29			30			31			32			33			34			35		
36			37			38			39			40			41			42		
43			44						45						46					
47			48						49						50					
51			52						53						54					
						g	h					m	n					s	t	
						e	f					k	l					q	r	
	c	d				i	j					o	p					u	v	
	E	I				S	N					T	F					J	P	

73

Follow These Steps to Finalize Your Temperament Identification

1. Read the descriptions of the temperaments that follow and select the temperament that is most like you. You may find that not all the aspects of a temperament truly reflect who you are. That's not uncommon. We are individuals and all are a little different, so what you are looking for is which of the four descriptions fits you best. Which is most like you?
2. You may find that you see a little of yourself in several or all of the temperaments. Don't worry. We all imitate others and therefore "borrow" strengths and characteristics from other temperaments for many reasons, not least to meet what others demand of us. What we need to know is which temperament we really are? As the research indicates we are one temperament, not a mixture of temperaments, and those glimpses of ourselves in other temperaments are simply our adopted strengths. Borrowed strengths or characteristics are just that, borrowed. Our own strengths are the ones that satisfy and fulfill us when we use them. We must know them.
3. Does the one that fits you best agree with your temperament key results? The two letters of the temperament you have chosen must occur in the four letters that your temperament key gave you. If they do, no further decision is needed.
4. If they don't, then you can go back and check your answers to the temperament key. Are they really what your preferences are and not what others have led you to believe you are or what you would like to be based on expectations others have given you? Make sure you answered the questions as instructed. A small number of people who take the temperament key may find it doesn't seem to ring true with who they perceive they are from

reading the descriptions.   If so, go with what you perceive is the temperament that fits you best.

The Four Temperaments

SP

They crave action, excitement, and stimulation, be it in sport, physical skills with the use of tools of all kinds, the performing arts, or even fine art. They are after a "good time" and only the introverted ones can happily sit still. SPs love freedom and act spontaneously; therefore, they do not take to authority with relish. Possessing a natural talent for all things physical, they can be the world's playmates. They are lovable, exciting, adventuresome, and brave risk-takers.

SPs are pleasant, tactical, and squeeze the last drop of excitement out of each moment. Adaptable, carefree, optimistic, individualistic, they crave self expression. Tolerance accompanies competitiveness and a generous spirit is usually seen in them.

Does this describe you best?

SJ

They are hard-working (many are workaholics) with a responsible work ethic, and they crave a feeling of security, which makes them somewhat cautious in their adventures. They coined the motto "Be prepared," and they like everything in order. Home, family, and responsibilities, all cast around rules and regulations. This makes them feel comfortable. They are the solid citizens and the backbone of society. They feel a sense of duty and feel drawn to be useful (helpmates). If someone does not do their duty it irks them.

Change can be unnerving and security is paramount if they are to be happy. They are more conservative than the SP and they like to feel in control of their world. They tend more to worry and pessimism rather than an optimistic attitude that all will be well. They must struggle to ensure all is well. Their nature is more serious and they are the guardians of society.

Does this describe you best?

NT

We could call this one the ingenious/technology temperament, although everyone craves the benefits of technology these days. They are curious and inventive, often finding their way into science and engineering occupations. NTs want to understand everything and build things. Often they are driven and compulsive, but display few people skills naturally. They are hard-working if what they are doing interests them. Feelings are not worn on the surface. NTs want to find new ways of doing things.

Facts, theories, strategies fill their minds and fuel their determination and focus. All things logical and only what makes sense guides them. They must feel independent, calm, cool, and intelligent. Scientific inquiry, mathematical, precision, and logical consistency in a skeptical mind describes them well. NTs are "mindmates."

Does this describe you best?

NF

They care very deeply about people and their world and want to lead people to their potential and to feelings of wholeness. NFs are very passionate, tender, loving, soulmates who want to please. Their inner world is frustrated with struggles, and they are the influencers of society, often finding their way into higher education (as do the NTs) and into teaching, counseling, and personal growth. They champion causes that benefit society and provide for the betterment of humankind. They long to better themselves together with the aforementioned urge to help others be all that they can be. They are emotionally rich and complicated and are easily hurt with their emotions very near the surface.

NFs are influencers, empathetic, passionate, emotional, sensitive, introspective, and lovers of harmony among people. Mostly they are perfectionists, self demanding, idealists, imaginative, and visionaries living in the world of dreams both practical and fanciful. To these self-actualizers, life must have meaning and significance.

Does this describe you best?

If you are still puzzled or unsure of which temperament you are and which describes you best, then go to my book, *INNERKINETICS®*, and all should soon become clear.

About the Author

Ray W. Lincoln is the bestselling author of *I May Frustrate You, but **I'm a Keeper*** and is the founder of Ray W. Lincoln & Associates. Ray's is a professional life coach and an expert in human nature. His 40 plus years of experience in speaking, teaching, and counseling began in New Zealand and have carried him professionally to Australia and the United States. He speaks with energy and enthusiasm before large and small audiences.

It was not by accident that he became the international speaker and coach that he is today and acquired the ability to guide so many to a happier, healthier, more fulfilled life. Ray has studied extensively in the fields of Philosophy, Temperament Psychology, and Personology.

A member of the National Speakers Association, his expertise has been used as a lecturer and professor, teacher and keynote speaker, seminar presenter, counselor, and coach. He teaches and leads in staff trainings, university student retreats, and parents' educational classes, as well as other seminars and training events. He also trains and mentors teachers, executives , and other professionals — all with the goal of understanding our own temperaments and those of others.

Ray lives with his wife, Mary Jo, in Littleton, Colorado where they enjoy hiking, snowshoeing, fly fishing, and all the beauty the Rocky Mountains offer. Both are highly involved in their work (which they feel is the most important and most fulfilling work of their entire career lives), both filling the roles for which they were designed, as they travel to speak to groups and to present seminars and workshops throughout the US.

Our website, www.raywlincoln.com, is a great place to order additional copies of:
- **I May Frustrate You, But I'm a Keeper**
- **INNERKINETICS**
- **A Journey Through Fear to Confidence**
- **Introduction to Faith and the Temperaments**
- **The InnerKinetics of Type**
- **Intelligently Emotional**
- **Your Child's Emotional World, Parts 1 and 2**

We also have additional FREE resources to help you. On our website you can:
- Sign up for our FREE monthly newsletter, which entitles you to receive 15% off all purchases at www.innerkinetics.com, www.imakeeperkid.com , and www.raywlincoln.com.
- Find more helpful resources and information about our services.

OUR SERVICES INCLUDE

Professional Life Coaching
Educational Seminars and Training
Keynote Addresses
Educational Materials
Free Monthly Newsletter

9 780996 120807